T0402838

MYTHICAL CREATURES

FUSION

MERMAIDS

by

Charis Mather

BEARPORT
PUBLISHING

Minneapolis, Minnesota

Credits

All images are courtesy of Shutterstock.com, unless otherwise specified. With thanks to Getty Images, Thinkstock Photo, and iStockphoto.

Recurring images – natashanast, Macrovector, sakurajia, holaillustrations, Sabelskaya, Neliakott. Cover – natashanast, Macrovector, sakurajia, holaillustrations, Sabelskaya, Neliakott. 4–5 – Alex Pix, tomertu. 6–7 – M.KOS, Poznyakov, SaltedLife. 8–9 – rudall30, Ironika. 10–11 – WarmWorld, Willyam Bradberry, Liu zishan. 12–13 – Martina Orlich, Olly Molly, Andriy Nekrasov, Ethan Daniels, wrangel. 14–15 – Catmando, nickolai_self_taught, TreesTons, Shift Space. 16–17 – amedved, vkilikov, Firn, Andrea Izzotti. 18–19 – Ian Dyball, Ludmila Meshcheriakova. 20–21 – EB Adventure Photography, Warm_Tail. 22–23 – Alfira, 23 estudio.

Bearport Publishing Company Product Development Team

President: Jen Jenson; Director of Product Development: Spencer Brinker; Managing Editor: Allison Juda; Associate Editor: Naomi Reich; Associate Editor: Tiana Tran; Senior Designer: Colin O'Dea; Associate Designer: Elena Klinkner; Associate Designer: Kayla Eggert; Product Development Assistant: Owen Hamlin

Library of Congress Cataloging-in-Publication Data

Names: Mather, Charis, 1999- author.
Title: Mermaids / by Charis Mather.
Description: Fusion books. | Minneapolis, Minnesota : Bearport Publishing Company, [2024] | Series: Mythical creatures | "This edition is published by arrangement with BookLife Publishing"--T.p. verso.
Identifiers: LCCN 2023030960 (print) | LCCN 2023030961 (ebook) | ISBN 9798889163039 (library binding) | ISBN 9798889163084 (paperback) | ISBN 9798889163121 (ebook)
Subjects: LCSH: Mermaids--Juvenile literature.
Classification: LCC GR910 .M36 2024 (print) | LCC GR910 (ebook) | DDC 398.21--dc23/eng/20230712
LC record available at https://lccn.loc.gov/2023030960
LC ebook record available at https://lccn.loc.gov/2023030961

For more information, write to Bearport Publishing, 5357 Penn Avenue South, Minneapolis, MN 55419.

CONTENTS

MYTHS, MAGIC, AND MORE

Most people have heard of the half-human, half-fish creatures known as mermaids. But you probably haven't seen one in real life. Why not? Because mermaids are **mythical** creatures!

For thousands of years, sailors all around the world have told stories about mermaids. Different **myths** talk about these creatures in different ways. Let's learn what the stories have to say!

The word *mermaid* is formed from two old English words that mean sea and woman.

WHAT DOES A MERMAID LOOK LIKE?

Let's take a closer look at these underwater creatures.

Fin

A large, wide fin helps mermaids swim. Sometimes, this fin is called a fluke.

Hair

Most mermaids
from stories
have long hair.

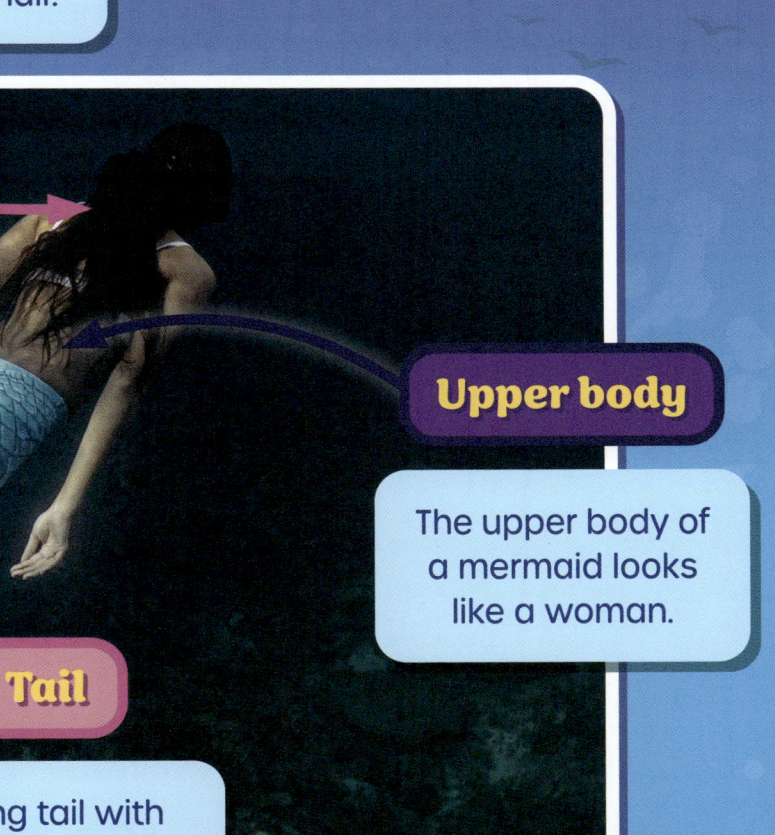

Upper body

The upper body of
a mermaid looks
like a woman.

Tail

A long tail with
scales makes up
this creature's
lower half.

THE TAIL

Mermaids are known to live their lives swimming below the waves. But could these creatures walk on land, too?

Some stories tell of mermaids growing legs and coming on land. Could there be mermaids walking among us without us knowing?

In stories, a mermaid's tail can **transform** into a pair of legs. But the mythical creatures have to be careful. If mermaids on land get wet, their feet become fins again.

BAD LUCK

Apart from being able to transform, what else have we heard about these mythical creatures? Mermaids are excellent singers.

Some say mermaids use their beautiful singing to **lure** sailors into the water. Once sailors hear the powerful mermaid song, they can't stop listening.

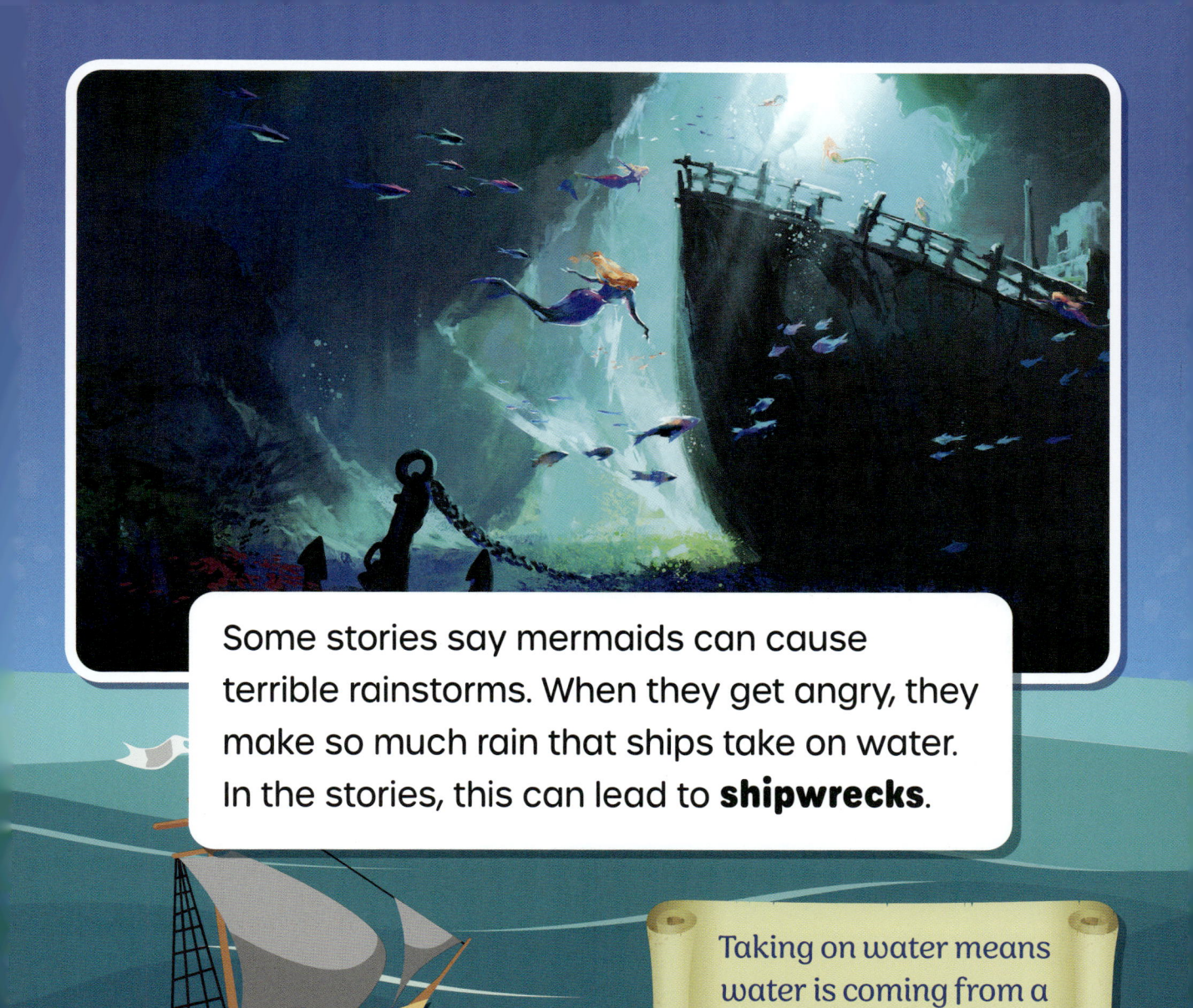

Some stories say mermaids can cause terrible rainstorms. When they get angry, they make so much rain that ships take on water. In the stories, this can lead to **shipwrecks**.

Taking on water means water is coming from a hole in the ship.

THIS AND THAT

Stories say mermaids can live for hundreds of years. Could that be possible? Maybe! Some sturgeon fish can live more than 100 years.

A sturgeon fish

Mermaids are said to collect beautiful things, such as corals or **pearls**. Many birds also collect shiny things to bring back to their nests.

Mermaids in stories can breathe under water. Fish don't need to swim up for air, either. Instead, they use their **gills** to breathe.

MERMEN

Could a half-fish, half-man exist as well? Some stories say mermen live among mermaids. Together, these mythical creatures are known as merfolk.

One of the most famous mermen is Triton. In stories, he is the son of a sea god. Triton can control the sea with his shell trumpet.

Triton

Triton's father is the god of earthquakes, horses, and the sea.

WHERE MERMAIDS LIVE

Mermaids live in the water, of course. But where exactly are they? Some say they can be found sitting on rocks poking out from the waves.

Or maybe merfolk live on the seafloor. Some stories say these fishy creatures live in cities under the water.

MYTHICAL LOOK-ALIKES

There are other mythical creatures like mermaids. Let's look at a few.

A siren

Sirens are half-human, half-bird creatures. Like mermaids, sirens lure sailors with their singing. This distracts sailors and makes them crash their boats.

When in the water, selkies are mythical creatures that look very similar to seals. But once they get on land, they change into humans. All they have to do is take off their seal coats!

A selkie?

The word *selkie* comes from the Scottish word for gray seal.

REAL-LIFE MERMAIDS?

Where do the stories of mermaids come from? Maybe from real animals. . . .

Dugongs

Dugongs are real underwater creatures. Like mermaids, they have flukes that help them swim.

Manatees

Manatees were sometimes mistaken for mermaids when sailors saw them from far away. These slow-moving creatures usually swim only about 5 miles per hour (8 kph).

MYSTERIOUS MYTHICAL CREATURES

Mermaids are fun, mysterious creatures. We can learn a lot from stories about these magical beings.

If you can't get enough of mermaids, just read some books! There is so much to learn about these magical, mythical creatures.

GLOSSARY

gills body parts that help fish breathe underwater

lure to attract or lead someone into a trap

mythical based on stories or something made up in the imagination

myths old stories that tell of strange or magical events and creatures

pearls hard, shiny balls that are sometimes found in shells and can be used as jewelry

scales small, hard skin parts found on animals such as fish and snakes

shipwrecks the destruction or loss of ships

transform to change into something else

INDEX